Early TRANSPORTATION Encyclopedias

TRUCKS

by Mari Bolte

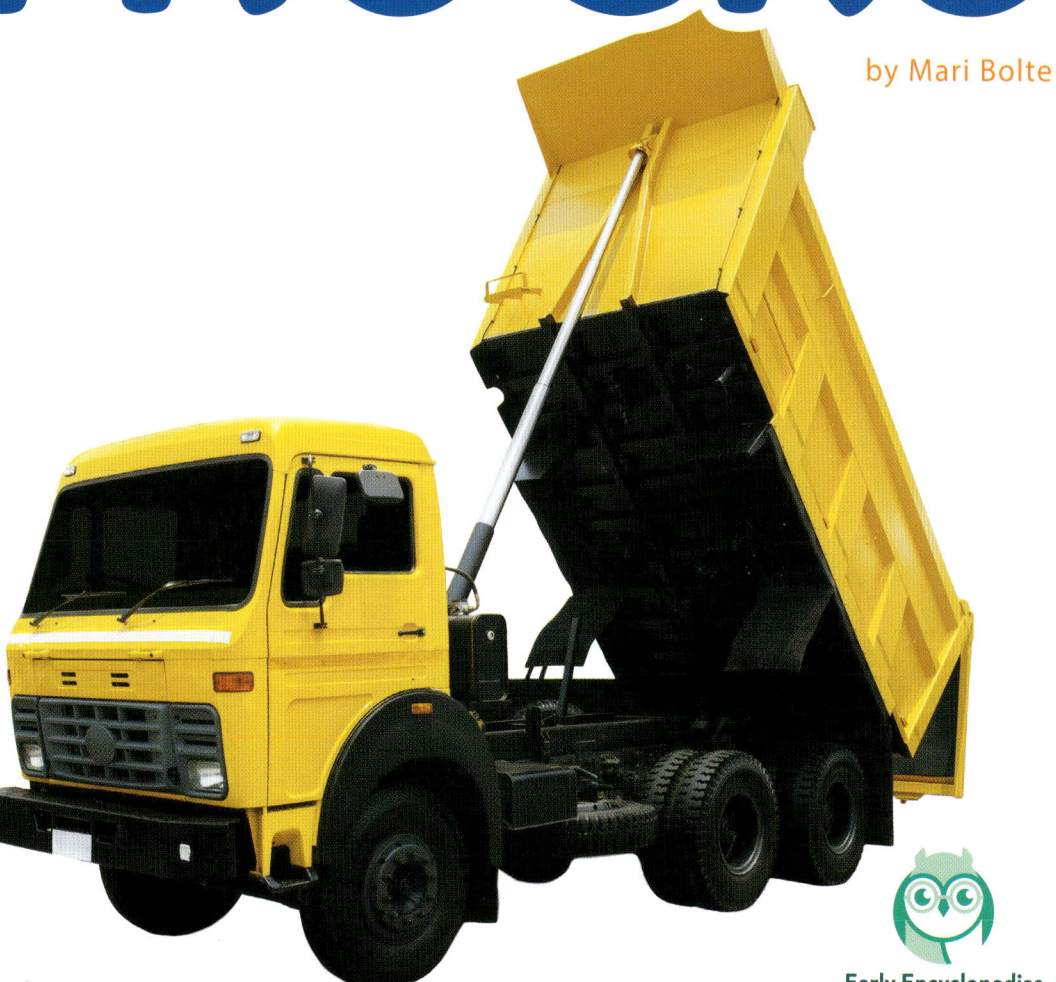

Early Encyclopedias

An Imprint of Abdo Reference
abdobooks.com

NEW HANOVER COUNTY PUBLIC LIBRARY

abdobooks.com

Published by Abdo Reference, a division of ABDO, PO Box 398166, Minneapolis, Minnesota 55439. Copyright © 2024 by Abdo Consulting Group, Inc. International copyrights reserved in all countries. No part of this book may be reproduced in any form without written permission from the publisher. Early Encyclopedias™ is a trademark and logo of Abdo Reference.
Printed in China
102023
012024

Editor: Carrie Hasler
Series Designer: Candice Keimig

Library of Congress Control Number: 2023939628

Publisher's Cataloging-in-Publication Data

Names: Bolte, Mari, author.
Title: Trucks / by Mari Bolte
Description: Minneapolis, Minnesota : Abdo Reference, 2024 | Series: Early transportation encyclopedias | Includes online resources and index.
Identifiers: ISBN 9781098292966 (lib. bdg.) | ISBN 9798384910909 (ebook)
Subjects: LCSH: Trucks--Juvenile literature. | Automobiles--Juvenile literature. | Lorries (Motor vehicles)--Juvenile literature. | Vehicles--Juvenile literature. | Transportation--Juvenile literature. | Encyclopedias and dictionaries--Juvenile literature.
Classification: DDC 629.224--dc23

CONTENTS

Introduction 4
Parts of a Truck 6
Timeline 8
    Construction Trucks 10
    Emergency Trucks 24
    Everyday Trucks 36
    Futuristic Trucks 52
    Jobsite Trucks 58
    Sports Trucks 76
    Super Heavy Trucks 86
    Transportation Trucks 94
    Unusual Trucks 110
Glossary 126
To Learn More 127
Index 127
Photo Credits 128

INTRODUCTION

Let's Get Truckin'

They move things from here to there. They bring us the things we need. What are they? Trucks!

Before trucks, horses pulled wagons full of supplies. But horses had weight limits. Trains also carried goods. But trains only traveled to large cities.

The first truck was invented by Gottlieb Daimler in 1896. He showed that his truck could stand up to heavy work every day.

In 1925, Henry Ford started selling pickup trucks. His truck was faster than horses. The trucks didn't need food. They did not get tired. Today, trucks are used around the world.

FUN FACT!

Early drivers did not have stop signs, speed limits, or traffic lights. The road was a dangerous place!

PARTS OF A TRUCK

Parts of a Truck

Trucks fill many roles. Drivers use trucks to bring items to stores. People drive trucks to work. Construction trucks carry heavy loads. Emergency trucks dash down the road. They help people in need. Unusual trucks do specific jobs. Some drive off-road or through the water. Futuristic trucks might drive themselves. They might even drive on the moon!

There are many different trucks, and each one does something different!

Engine: creates power that makes the truck go

Chassis: the truck's skeleton

Tires: part of the wheels

There are many different parts of a truck. Each part is important!

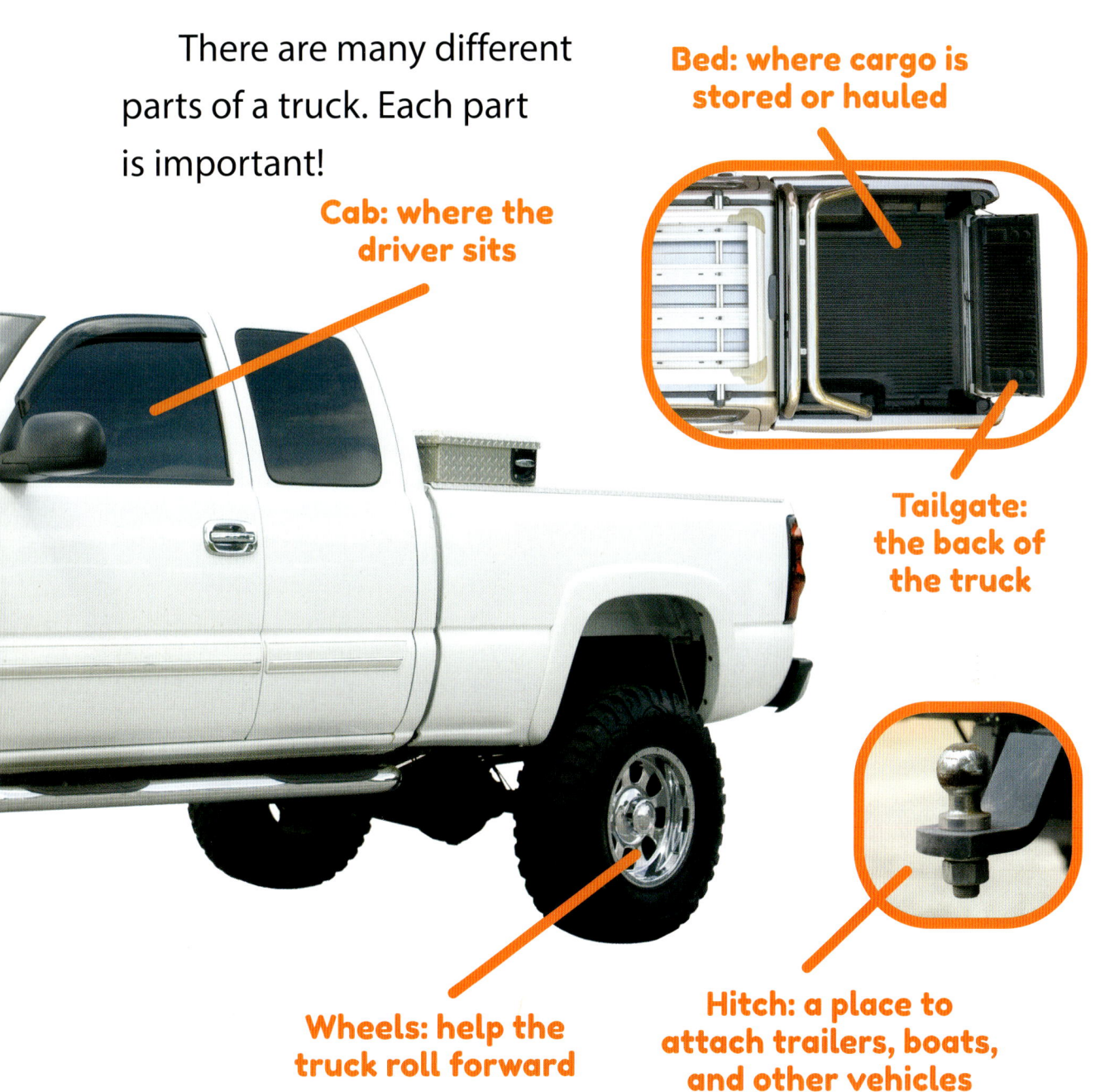

Cab: where the driver sits

Bed: where cargo is stored or hauled

Tailgate: the back of the truck

Wheels: help the truck roll forward

Hitch: a place to attach trailers, boats, and other vehicles

TIMELINE

1896: Daimler Motor-Lastwagen was the first truck on the market.

1905: The first gas-powered ambulance was introduced. It had three wheels. Its sides were bulletproof.

1910: Trucks became popular for making deliveries.

1916: Ernest Holmes built the Holmes Wrecker. It was the world's first tow truck.

1925: Ford's Model T Runabout with a pickup bed was the first factory-built pickup.

1937: The first aircraft rescue firefighting (ARFF) vehicle was built. It could fight fires at airports.

1948: The first Ford F-Series hit the market. It was the best-selling truck every year starting in 1976.

1983: AM General won a contract from the US Army. They would build High Mobility Multipurpose Wheeled Vehicles.

2008: A copper mine in Chile began using self-driving trucks.

2021: The Rivian R1T was the first all-electric truck to hit the market.

CONSTRUCTION TRUCKS

Concrete Mixers

Construction trucks move dirt, rocks, and other heavy things. Their job is hard!

Concrete mixers are one type of construction truck. Concrete is hard to stir. It's also heavy to move. A concrete mixer can do both of those things.

Length:
20 to 30 feet
(6.1 to 9.1 m)

Width:
8 feet
(2.4 m)

Height:
13 feet
(4 m)

Weight, Loaded:
66,000 pounds
(29,937.1 kg)

FUN FACT! Concrete is poured into place using a slide.

A drum on the back of the truck spins. Cement powder is poured in. Water and rocks are added. Blades inside the drum stir everything.

The truck brings the concrete to the jobsite. It mixes on the way. When the drum is mixing, it spins one way. When the concrete is ready, it spins the other way.

CONSTRUCTION TRUCKS

Concrete Pump Trucks

Sometimes concrete is needed in places where a truck can't go. Workers might need concrete to make a pool in someone's backyard. But how does it get there? Concrete pump trucks can help!

Some trucks have a special arm. This is called a boom. The boom can move in any direction. A driver controls it. The pump pushes concrete through the boom.

FUN FACT!
Dried concrete can be removed from hoses with water or air pressure.

Other trucks have a hose. A pump pushes concrete through the hose. Hoses are easy to move and control. Workers can pour concrete in backyards or long alleys.

Length:
36.5 feet
(11.1 m)

Width:
8.2 feet
(2.5 m)

Weight:
54,600 pounds
(24,766 kg)

Boom Length:
65 to 200 feet
(20 to 61 m)

CONSTRUCTION TRUCKS

Crane Trucks

Crane trucks are used to load and move things. They have a metal arm on their back that stretches. Some arms stretch as tall as an 18-story building. When its job is done, the arm is pulled in. The truck can drive away safely.

FUN FACT!
Crane trucks are also called boom trucks.

Crane trucks have different parts for different jobs. The parts can be switched out. Drills make holes in the ground. Grapples grab and lift things. Forks lift flat items. Buckets can be filled with dirt or stone. Powerful magnets lift cars or sheets of metal.

Length:
36 to 44 feet
(11 to 13.4 m)

Lifting Weight:
6,000 to 80,000 pounds
(2,721.6 to 36,287.4 kg)

Width:
21 to 24 feet
(6.4 to 7.3 m)

Arm Length:
100 to 200 feet
(30.5 to 61 m)

CONSTRUCTION TRUCKS

Dump Trucks

Dirt, sand, and trash are hard to move. They fall through cracks. They blow away. Dump trucks are the answer!

Length:
24.5 feet
(7.5 m)

Weight:
26,000 to 30,000 pounds
(11,793.4 to 13,607.8 kg)

Width:
8.5 feet
(2.6 m)

Load Size, in Pounds:
13,000 to 28,000 pounds
(5,896.7 to 12,700.6 kg)

FUN FACT! Hydraulics can easily lift hundreds, or even thousands, of pounds.

The first dump wagon was invented in May 1884. It looked like an ordinary wagon. But the front of the wagon could tip up with a motor. Anything in the wagon would fall out on its own. Today's dump trucks use hydraulics to lift the trucks' beds and dump out loads.

A dump truck's hydraulic cylinder

CONSTRUCTION TRUCKS

Dump Trucks

There are many different dump trucks. Standard dump trucks are the most common. One end of their box lifts in the air. The load falls out.

Transfer trucks are also dump trucks. They pull a box behind them. The box is moved to the main truck to be dumped.

FUN FACT! Dump trucks can tip over if the load does not come out smoothly or if the ground is uneven.

Bottom dump trucks let their loads out from the bottom. They do not tip at all.

Side dump trucks tilt to one side or the other. Their loads spill out fast.

Bottom dump truck

Did You Know?

Tri-axle dump trucks can haul heavier loads. They have extra wheels. When the truck doesn't have a load, the extra wheels don't touch the road.

Tri-axle dump truck

19

CONSTRUCTION TRUCKS

Super Dump Trucks

Dump trucks come in many sizes. Super dump trucks can haul as much as transfers or doubles. Some can haul twice as much. They are also faster. This is because all the load can be dumped at once.

Length:
34 to 40 feet
(10.4 to 12.2 m)

Width:
8.5 feet
(2.6 m)

Weight:
29,600 pounds
(13,426.3 kg)

Load Size:
38,000 to 52,000 pounds
(17,236.5 to 23,586.8 kg)

Off-highway dump trucks do not drive on the road. They work in mines. They also haul heavy loads of dirt.

How Much Can They Carry?

20 tons
(18.1 metric tons)

30 tons
(27.2 metric tons)

40 tons
(36.3 metric tons)

CONSTRUCTION TRUCKS

Haul Trucks

Haul trucks don't drive on roads. They are too big. Mines and quarries need big trucks, though. Haul trucks move construction equipment from one place to the other. They also carry heavy rocks and coal.

BelAZ 75710

The BelAZ 75710 is the world's biggest haul truck. It is as long as two school buses! It can carry 496 tons (450 metric tons).

Regular big dump trucks have six tires. The BelAZ 75710 has eight. And they are huge! An adult human wouldn't even come halfway up one of the tires.

FUN FACT! The largest BelAZ 75710 wheel is 13 feet (4 m) across.

Length:
68 feet
(20.7 m)

Width:
32 feet
(9.8 m)

Weight:
720,000 pounds
(326,586.5 kg)

Height:
27 feet
(8.2 m)

23

EMERGENCY TRUCKS

Ambulances

Out of the way! There's an emergency! Ambulances are one kind of emergency truck. The first ambulance was built in 1899. But trucks were faster. They could carry more equipment too.

Did You Know?
The words on the front of emergency vehicles are backward. They look normal in rearview mirrors.

Today, ambulances still bring patients to hospitals. But they can also help at the scene of the emergency. Paramedics ride inside. They are ready for anything.

FUN FACT!

Before ambulances, horses and wagons carried patients to hospitals.

Type 1 Ambulance

Length: 24 feet (7.3 m)

Width: 8 feet (2.4 m)

Height: 9 feet (2.7 m)

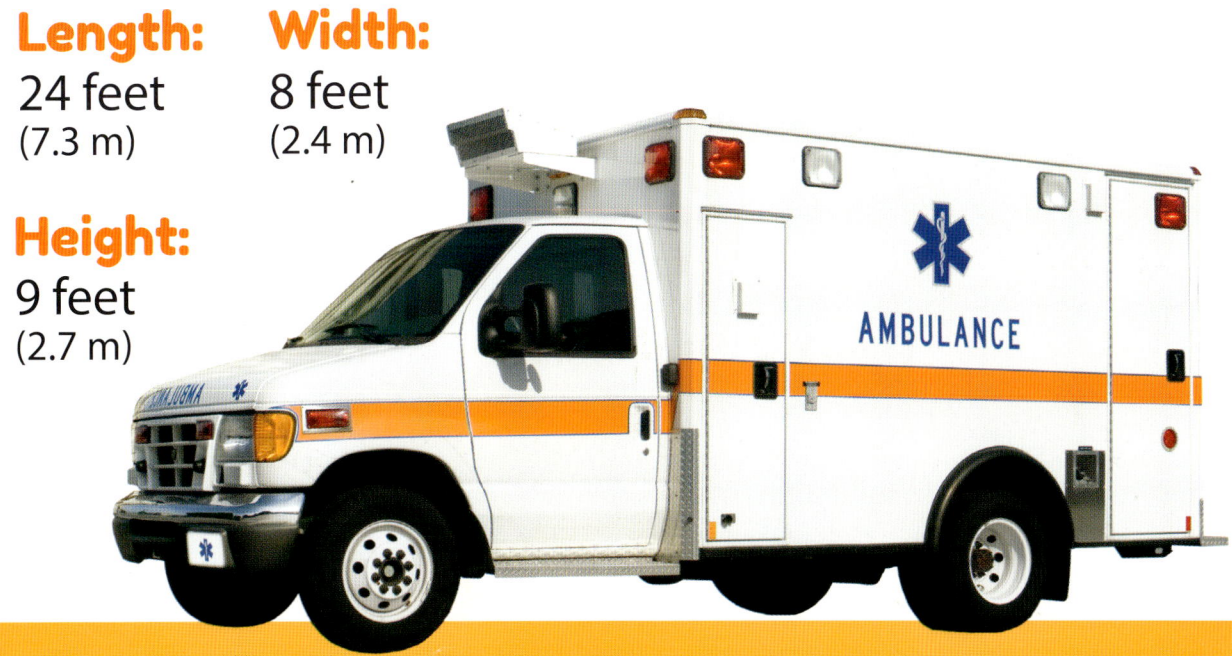

EMERGENCY TRUCKS

Ambulances

There are three types of ambulance. Each has its own job.

Type 1 are a lot like pickup trucks. This is the most common style. The driver sits in the cab. A small window lets the driver talk to people in the back.

> **Did You Know?**
> The fastest ambulance in the world can reach speeds of 245 miles per hour (394.3 kmh).

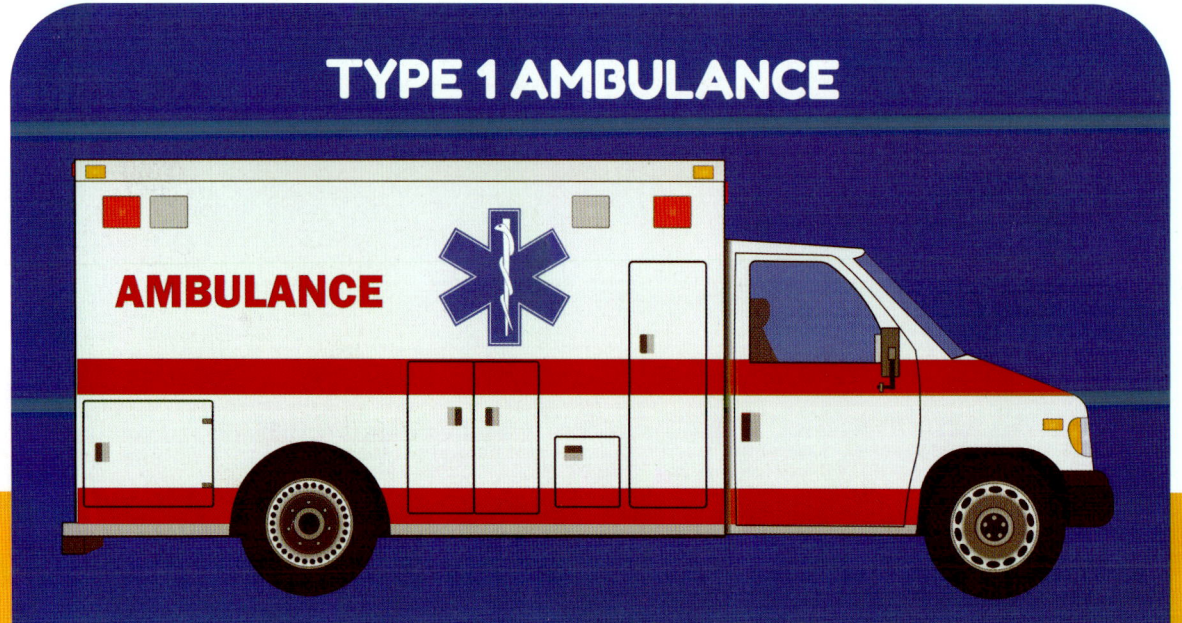

TYPE 1 AMBULANCE

TYPE 2 AMBULANCE

Type 2 looks like vans. They give people rides from one hospital to another. They also help out in emergencies.

Type 3 looks a lot like Type 1. The cab and the back are connected, though. People can easily move between the front and the back.

TYPE 3 AMBULANCE

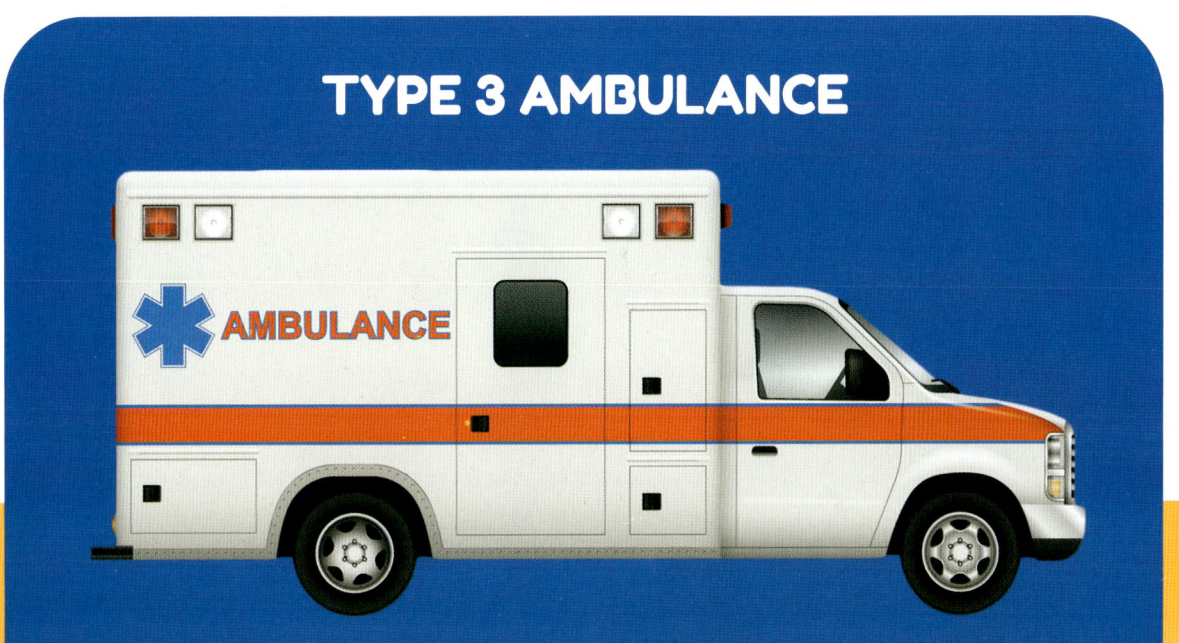

EMERGENCY TRUCKS

Firefighting Trucks

Did you know that there are actually two kinds of firefighting trucks? There are fire trucks and fire engines.

Fire trucks have long ladders on the back. Some people call them ladder trucks. They can stretch to reach high places.

FUN FACT!
Fire-engine red is actually not the safest color for emergency vehicles. Fluorescent colors, like bright yellow, are!

The longest ladder is called an aerial. It can reach 100 feet (30.5 m) in the air.

Some fire trucks have a boom instead of a ladder. A basket or platform on the end can hold people or supplies.

Did You Know?
Some fires send dangerous gas into the air. Firefighting foam stops it from escaping.

Length:
24 to 35 feet
(7.3 to 10.7 m)

Width:
8 feet
(2.4 m)

Height:
9 to 12 feet
(2.7 to 3.7 m)

EMERGENCY TRUCKS

Fire Engines

Fire engines are different from fire trucks. Fire engines don't have big ladders. Instead, they carry hoses. The hoses spray water on the fire. Most fire engines hold between 300 and 750 gallons (1,135.6 to 2,839.1 L) of water. Some carry 1,000 gallons (3,785.4 L) or more!

FUN FACT! When you call 911, a fire truck and an ambulance are sent to help.

Some fire trucks can do both jobs. They can carry water. They can also have an attached ladder. But the firefighters might not use everything.

Did You Know?
Some fire trucks are called quints. *Quint* means "five." Quints store all five main tools a fire truck needs.

Ground ladder

Ladder

Quint

Fire hose

Water tank

Pump

EMERGENCY TRUCKS

Heavy Rescue Trucks

Accidents happen. Heavy rescue trucks can help! They can carry lots of equipment. If a bridge fails, ropes and chains can pull cars to safety. Heavy rescue trucks can get people out of danger fast.

Length: 43 feet (13.1 m)

Width: 8 feet (2.4 m)

Height: 12 feet (3.7 m)

Weight, Fully Loaded: more than 35,000 pounds (15,875.7 kg)

People who are lost or hurt must be found fast. Heavy rescue trucks help with search and rescue. Saws can cut trees or poles out of the way. Cranes lift searchers high in the air. They can see over trees or across rivers. When it gets dark, bright lights let the search keep going.

Did You Know?

The Jaws of Life are used to get people out of cars quickly. Other tools take an hour or more to remove a car roof. The Jaws of Life can do the job in about two minutes.

EMERGENCY TRUCKS

Snowplows

Snowstorms can shut whole cities down. Icy roads are dangerous. Thanks to snowplows, drivers can be back on the road in no time!

Many snowplows are dump trucks. Some are used to push snow. A shovel called a blade attaches to the front of the truck. These trucks clear the road.

FUN FACT!
Snowplows usually travel at speeds of 30 miles per hour (48.3 kmh) or less.

Some trucks clear the road and spread salt or sand. They make the road less slippery. A spreader goes onto the back of the bed. Spreaders toss the salt out in an even layer.

Length:
28 to 30 feet
(8.5 to 9.1 m)

Width:
10 to 13 feet
(3 to 4 m)

Height:
10 feet
(3 m)

Main Blade Width:
12 feet
(3.7 m)

Did You Know?

Snowplows can work together! Three or four plows spread across the road. They line up diagonally. Then they start driving. A group of plows can clear a whole road at once!

EVERYDAY TRUCKS

World's First Truck

In 1896, German Gottlieb Daimler showed off his wagon. It had wooden wheels. There was a bench for a driver. It looked like it was ready to be pulled by horses. But then it moved on its own!

Daimler Lastwagen

Years Made:
1896 to 1898

Length:
15 feet
(4.6 m)

Maximum Horsepower (Hp):
4 hp

Top Speed:
17.4 miles per hour
(28 kmh)

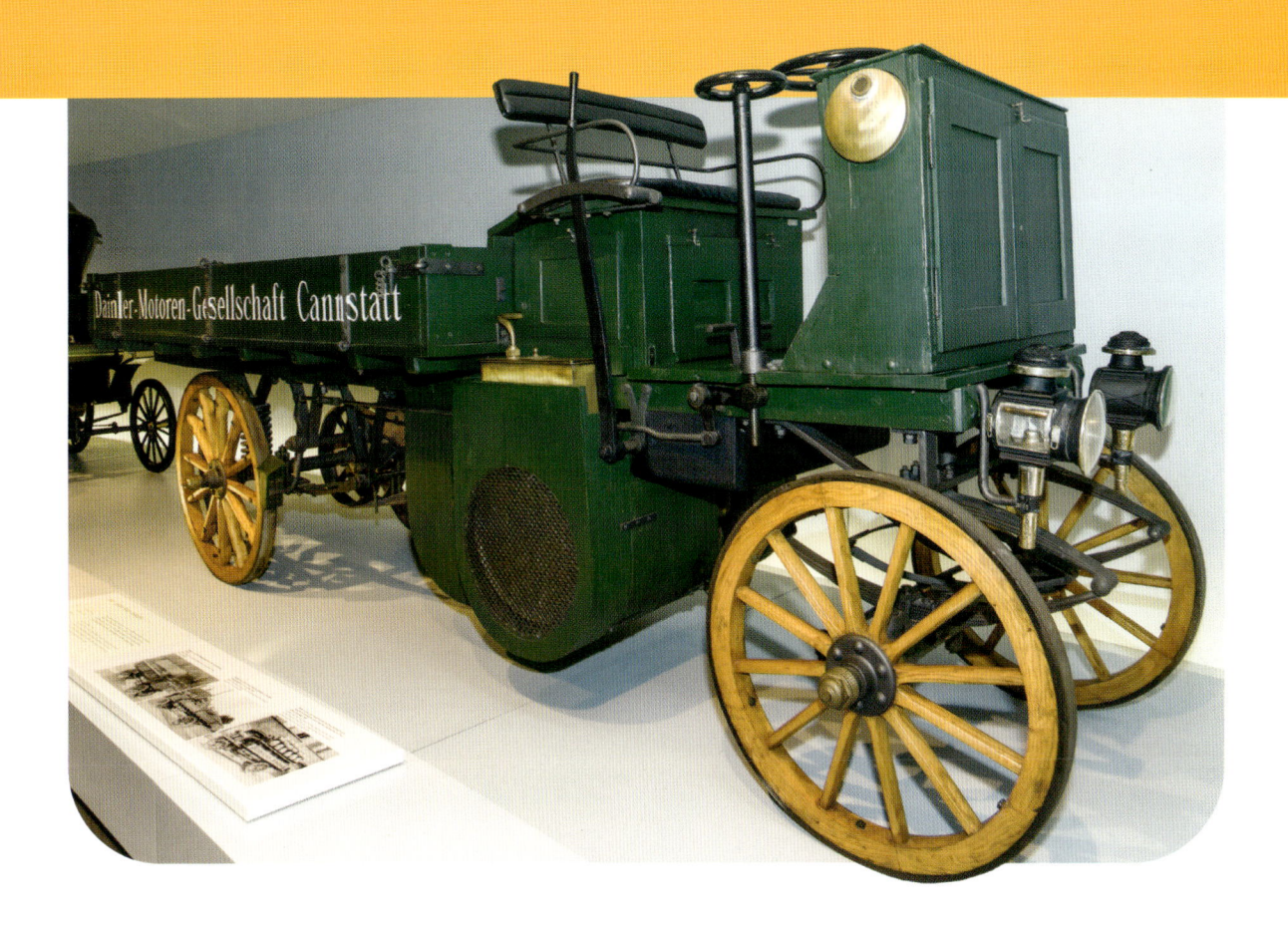

The Lastwagen was not fast. But it worked well for delivering heavy things. It could easily move through the city. And keeping a car was less expensive than keeping a horse.

Did You Know?

Daimler made more than cars. First, he invented the motorcycle. Then he made trolley cars. He also made a fire truck with a hose. In 1899, his company DMG built the first Mercedes car.

EVERYDAY TRUCKS

First Popular Trucks

The first truck was Ford's Model T Roadster with Pickup Body. Farmers were already using Model T Fords. They were used for field work. Farmers took out the back seats. They also added boxes to the back.

Model T

Model A

T Roadster with Pickup Body

In 1925, factories began selling the popular Model T trucks. The next version, the Model A, had greater horsepower. It became even more popular than the Model T.

Years Made:
1925 to 1927

Length:
11 feet
(3.4 m)

Maximum Hp:
20 hp

Top Speed:
42 miles per hour
(67.6 kmh)

FUN FACT! About 5 million Model As were made.

EVERYDAY TRUCKS

Crew Cab Pickups

Most of the pickup trucks you see on the road are called light trucks. Light trucks come in many different sizes. Crew cabs are the largest. They have four full-size doors and two rows of seats. For a long time, crew cabs were just used at jobsites.

FUN FACT! The first crew cab was the Travelette. It came out in 1957.

2020 Dodge Ram Longhorn

Crew cabs, like the Dodge Ram Longhorn, became popular with families. They can hold a lot of people and belongings.

Years Made:
2010 to present

Length:
20 feet (6.1 m)

Maximum Hp:
305 hp

Maximum Towing Capacity:
6,150 pounds (2,789.6 kg)

EVERYDAY TRUCKS

Electric Trucks

Most trucks are powered by gasoline or diesel. Electric cars and trucks use batteries instead. Some use both fuel and batteries.

The first electric vehicle was built in 1832. Electric trucks were used to deliver milk in the 1910s and 1920s. Short routes around the city worked well. The trucks could stop and charge their batteries anywhere.

Roads got better and gas was cheap. Electric trucks stopped being popular. But electric did not go away.

FUN FACT! With more electric vehicles on the road, many charging stations are being installed throughout the US.

Rivian R1T

In 2021, the Rivian R1T became the first modern all-electric truck.

Years Made:
2021 to present

Maximum Hp:
835 hp

Length:
18 feet
(5.5 m)

Top Speed:
112 miles per hour
(180.2 kmh)

EVERYDAY TRUCKS

Extended Cab Pickups

Extended cab pickups are like regular trucks with extra space. Some people call them double cabs. These trucks have two rows of seats. Two main doors open to the front seats. Sometimes the back seat is just a bench. Other times, there are small seats. They are called jump seats. Most can be folded down or flipped up for more storage space.

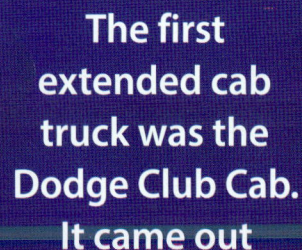

FUN FACT!
The first extended cab truck was the Dodge Club Cab. It came out in 1973.

2021 Toyota Tacoma Double Cab

Tacoma is the Coast Salish word for Mount Rainier in Washington. Toyota picked the name because they wanted their truck to seem powerful and strong. Toyota fans also call this truck the "Taco."

Years Made:
1995 to present

Maximum Hp:
278 hp

Length:
18 feet
(5.5 m)

Top Speed:
113 miles per hour
(182 kmh)

EVERYDAY TRUCKS

Mini Trucks

Japanese mini trucks are used around the world. They are smaller versions of regular pickups. Mini trucks carry props on movie sets. They can also deliver fruits and vegetables.

Mini trucks can be mini dump trucks. Mini snow plows push smaller amounts of ice and snow.

FUN FACT!
Japanese mini trucks are sometimes called kei trucks.

Mini trucks usually hold only two people. But mini crew cabs can get four people and their supplies anywhere they need to go.

Years Made:
1949 to present

Maximum Hp:
63 hp

Length:
11 feet
(3.4 m)

Top Speed:
75 miles per hour
(120.7 kmh)

EVERYDAY TRUCKS

Most Popular Trucks

The Ford F-Series was first made in 1948. Ford's models went from F-1 to F-8. The bigger the number, the more powerful the truck.

Ford F-Series

Years Made:
1948 to present

Length:
19 feet
(5.8 m)

Maximum Hp:
700 hp

Top Speed:
110 miles per hour
(177 kmh)

Maximum Weight Load:
4,700 pounds
(2,131.9 kg)

48

By 1975, the F-Series trucks were the best-selling trucks in America. They had nice seats and looked good. They had the newest technology. F-Series could hold up to tough jobs too. There was a truck for everyone.

Did You Know?

In the 1960s, Ford offered turn signals, heat, seat belts, and a radio. Not many cars had these back then!

EVERYDAY TRUCKS

Regular Cab Pickup Trucks

Regular cab pickups have only two doors. For many years, two-door pickup trucks were all people drove. There were no back seats. Until the 1980s, most pickups had a bench-style seat in the front. That meant three people could ride up front instead of two.

FUN FACT!

Toyota's first pickup was called the Stout. It came out in 1964.

50

2011 Chevrolet Silverado 1500

The Silverado was first made in 1999. It's been a very popular truck ever since. The 1500 in its name means it has a payload of 1,500 pounds (680.4 kg).

Years Made:
1999 to present

Length:
19 feet
(5.8 m)

Maximum Hp:
302 hp

Top Speed:
152 miles per hour
(244.6 kmh)

FUTURISTIC TRUCKS

Cybertrucks

The Tesla Cybertruck looks like something an alien would drive. The outside is made from shiny steel. It's also all electric. It can drive 500 miles (804.7 km) on one charge.

FUN FACT! The Cybertruck can drive itself!

The Cybertruck's bed is different. Tesla calls it a vault. The press of a button uncovers the vault. Another press covers it. Anything stored inside is protected. A built-in ramp makes it easy to load. The truck's bed can even be turned into a tent for camping!

Tesla Cybertruck

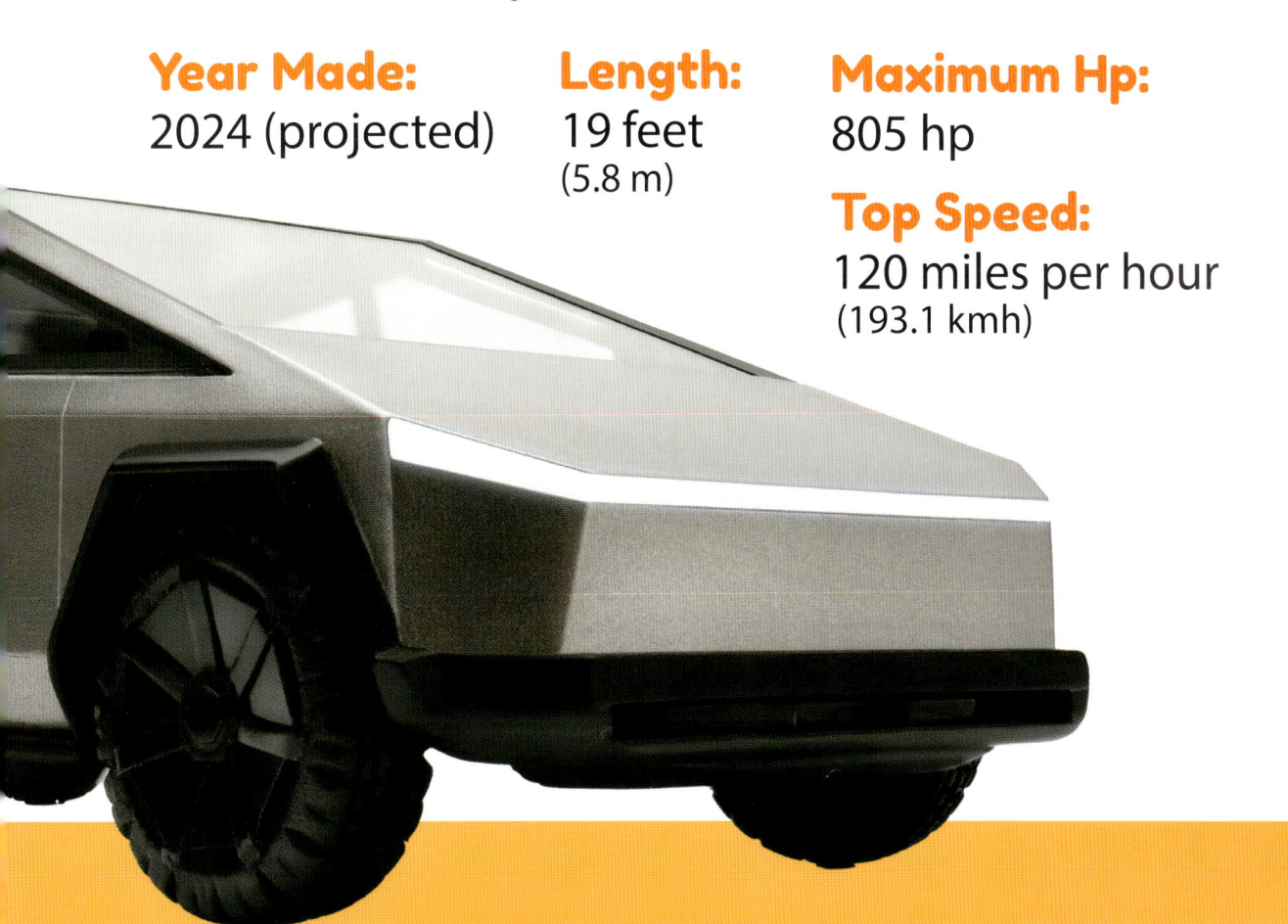

Year Made:
2024 (projected)

Length:
19 feet
(5.8 m)

Maximum Hp:
805 hp

Top Speed:
120 miles per hour
(193.1 kmh)

FUTURISTIC TRUCKS

Lunar Terrain Vehicle

NASA scientists want to send people back to the moon. And those people will need trucks! Trucks for the moon are called Lunar Terrain Vehicles (LTVs). In 2021, NASA put out a challenge. Who could build the next LTV?

NASA's Requirements

Passengers:
at least 2

Minimum Load Weight:
1,764 pounds (800.1 kg)

Top Speed:
9 miles per hour (14.5 kmh)

Minimum Travel Time:
8 hours

The LTV must be built to last. NASA hopes it can work for at least 10 years. Scientists back on Earth need to be able to drive the LTV. It also needs to work with robots that will be on the moon.

FUN FACT!
The LTV will be electric.

FUTURISTIC TRUCKS

Self-Driving Trucks

Some trucks drive themselves! The company TuSimple started with a truck on the roads of Arizona. Their trucks use cameras to "see."

In 2021, a test truck drove itself on an open, public road. Since then, it has driven more than 200,000 miles (321,868.8 km). A person must still ride inside the trucks on the road, though. This is for safety.

TuSimple Driverless Trucks

Did You Know?
There are different levels of self-driving cars. Some assist drivers. Other cars drive completely on their own.

Years Made:
2021 to present

Length:
70 feet
(21.3 m)

Top Speed:
75 miles per hour
(120.7 kmh)

JOBSITE TRUCKS

Armored Trucks

Money needs to be moved from one bank to another. Jewels are delivered to stores. Paintings are taken to museums. How do these things get there? Armored trucks!

Armored trucks carry valuables. They are built to keep things safe. No one can break in. The trucks have two armed guards.

FUN FACT!

The first Brink's armored vehicle was a school bus.

Brink's trucks are the most famous armored truck. The trucks are extra heavy. They have armor and thick glass. Bullets can't get through. They can even survive explosions. The doors lock automatically when they close.

Length:
24 feet
(7.3 m)

Width:
8 feet
(2.4 m)

Height:
10 feet
(3 m)

Armor Thickness:
more than 0.25 inches
(0.6 cm)

JOBSITE TRUCKS

Bucket Trucks

Bucket trucks are work trucks with a boom attached. They can lift people high in the air. They are sometimes called cherry pickers. Back in the early 1900s, people used them to harvest fruit. It didn't take long for people to see other uses for them.

Length: 21 feet (6.4 m)

Width: 7 feet (2.1 m)

Height: 7 feet (2.1 m)

Electric companies use them to fix poles and wires. Painters can get at hard-to-reach spaces. Window washers can clean high windows. Bucket trucks are steady. There is little danger to workers.

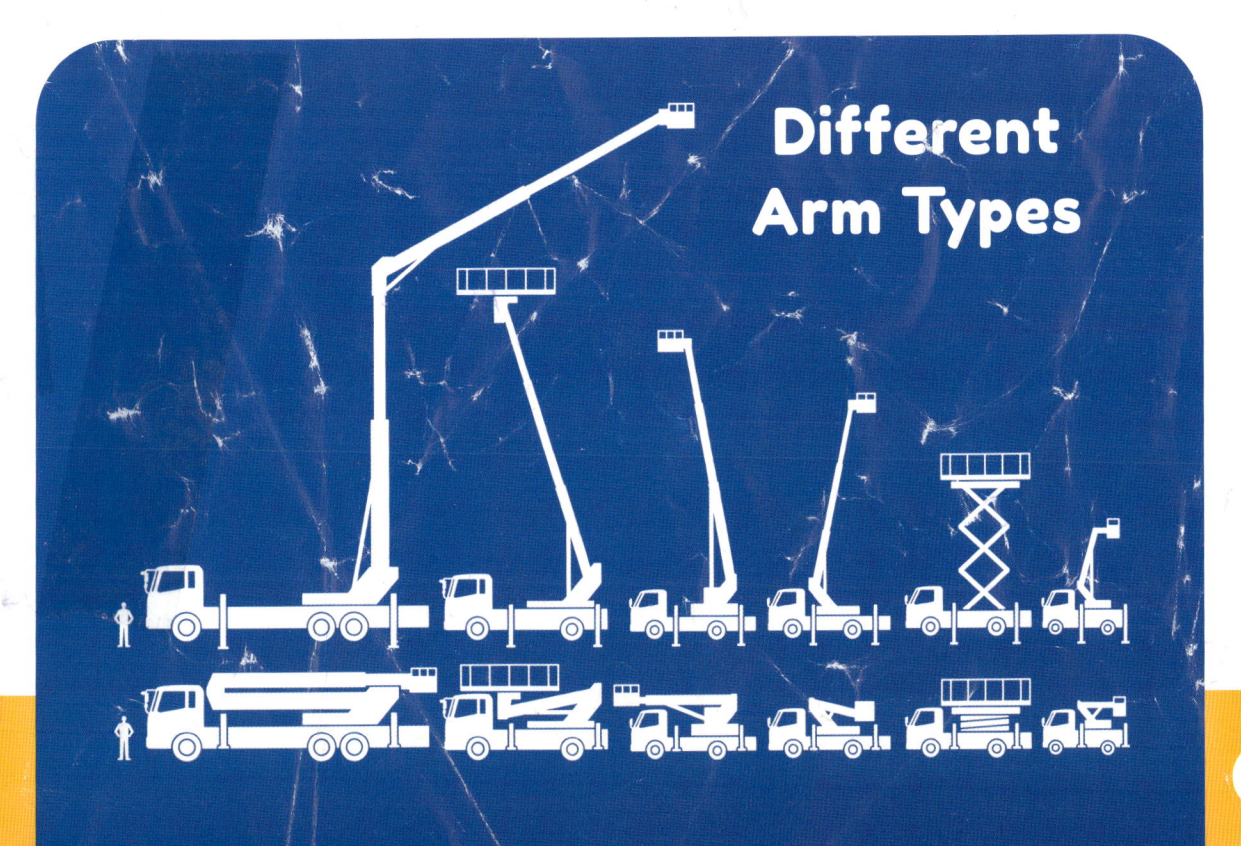

Different Arm Types

JOBSITE TRUCKS

Food Trucks

Food trucks are restaurants on wheels. The first food truck was the Wienermobile. It rolled onto city streets in 1936. It sold hot dogs. It also advertised Oscar Mayer wieners. By 2023, there were more than 36,000 food trucks across America.

FUN FACT!

Tacos, sandwiches, and French fries are some of the best-selling food truck treats.

Food trucks have fryers, stoves, and ovens for cooking. Refrigerators and freezers keep food fresh and drinks cold. There is room for people to work.

Did You Know?
In some cities, food truck parks have been built. People can try food from different trucks.

Wienermobile

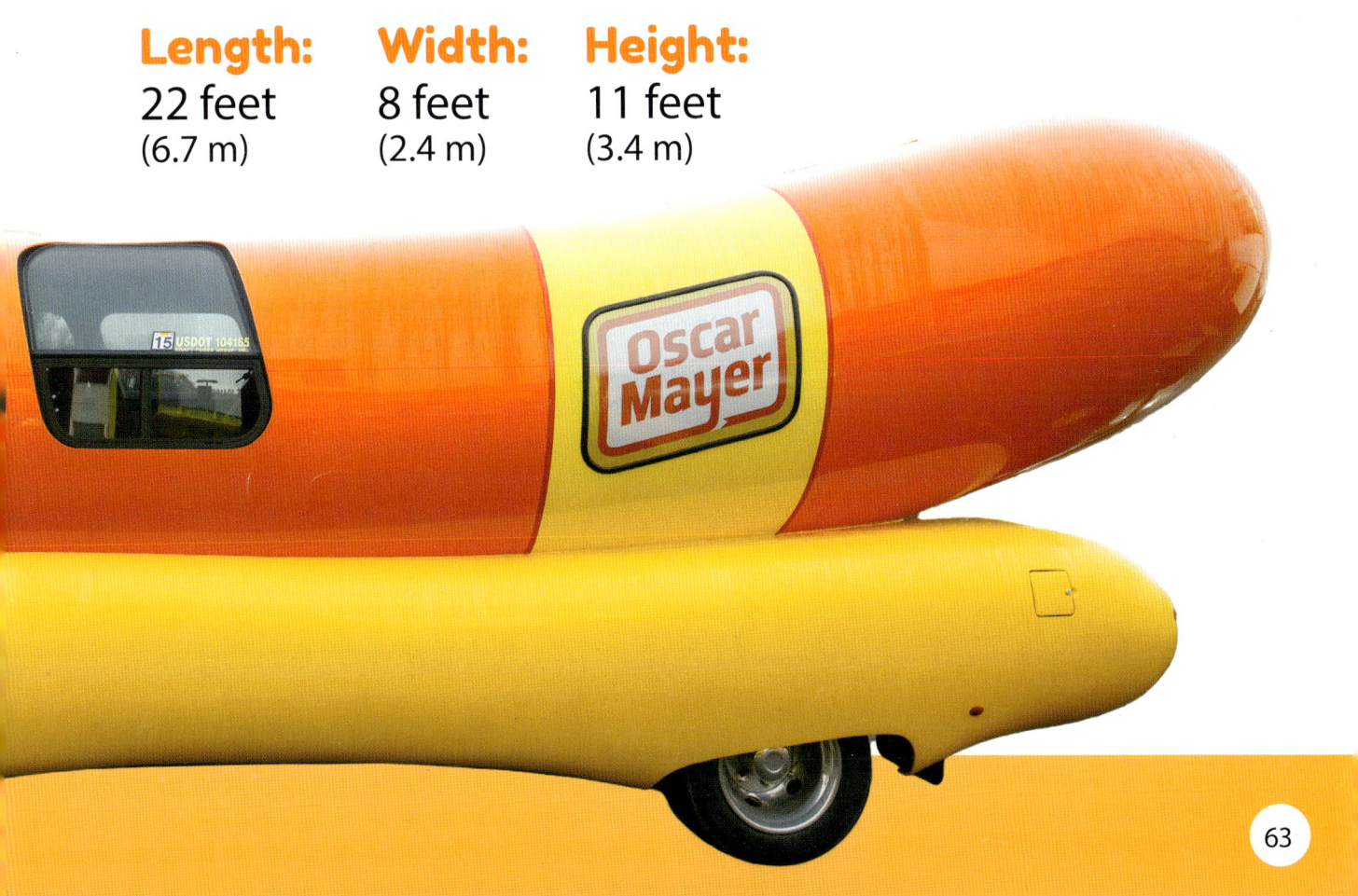

Length:
22 feet
(6.7 m)

Width:
8 feet
(2.4 m)

Height:
11 feet
(3.4 m)

JOBSITE TRUCKS

Forklifts

Forklifts are small trucks. They are used to lift and move things. They are used in warehouses and factories.

Being able to move things quickly and easily saves time. Forklifts can also help stack things. This saves space.

FUN FACT!
Forklifts have two sets of controls. One is for steering. The other is for lifting.

Forklifts are sometimes used at construction sites. They can move heavy stones. They can carry wood and supplies.

Did You Know?
Wooden pallets are used with forklifts. Loads sit on top of the pallets. There are spaces underneath. The forks on a forklift slide in. They lift and move the load.

Length:
8 to 10 feet
(2.4 to 3 m)

Width:
3 to 7 feet
(0.9 to 2.1 m)

Height:
7 to 15 feet
(2.1 to 4.6 m)

Lifting Power:
3,000 to 4,800 pounds
(1,360.8 to 2,177.2 kg)

JOBSITE TRUCKS

Garbage Trucks

Garbage trucks pick up trash. They take it to waste areas, landfills, and recycling centers.

Length:
19.5 to
23.5 feet
(5.9 to 7.2 m)

Width:
8.5 feet
(2.6 m)

Height:
12 feet
(3.7 m)

Load Weight:
20,000 to
36,000 pounds
(9,071.8 to 16,329.3 kg)

There are four different types of garbage trucks. Front loader trucks empty dumpsters. Side loaders and rear loaders pick up trash from houses. Roll off trucks drop off containers. The containers are filled with trash. Roll off trucks pick up containers when they are full.

JOBSITE TRUCKS

Grapple Trucks

Regular garbage trucks pick up trash cans. But some trash doesn't fit into a can. Logs, metal, and old building materials are too big and heavy. They might be falling apart or unsafe to handle. A grapple truck can lift them.

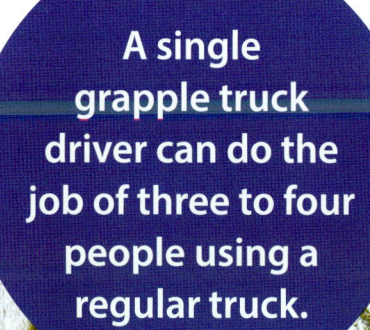

FUN FACT!
A single grapple truck driver can do the job of three to four people using a regular truck.

A grapple truck has a grappling claw. It is attached to a boom. The claw grabs the trash. It places it in the bed of the truck.

Did You Know?

More than 9 million freezers and refrigerators are thrown out in the United States every year. Grapple trucks make hauling them away easier.

Length:
up to 31 feet
(9.4 m)

Width:
8 feet
(2.4 m)

Height:
12 feet
(3.7 m)

Lift Height:
8 to 10 feet
(2.4 to 3 m)

JOBSITE TRUCKS

Tow Trucks

In 1916, Ernest Holmes got a car stuck in a creek. He spent all day trying to get it out. That gave him an idea. He invented the first tow truck! It was called the Holmes Wrecker.

There are three kinds of tow trucks: hook and chain, wheel lifts, and flatbeds.

Hook and chain trucks use hooks to pull cars. A wheel lift truck tows a car by two wheels. Flatbed trucks pull cars onto their bed. The car is fastened in place. Then the truck drives the car away.

FUN FACT!
Hook and chain trucks are also called wreckers.

Length:
19 to 48 feet
(5.8 to 14.6 m)

Height:
7 feet
(2.1 m)

Weight:
at least 10,000 pounds
(4,535.9 kg)

Towing Strength:
7,000 to 17,000 pounds
(3,175.1 to 7,711.1 kg)

JOBSITE TRUCKS

Vacuum Trucks

Sometimes garbage is in piles of dust. Other times, it's liquid. How can these get cleaned up? A vacuum truck can help with that!

FUN FACT!
Trucks that can vacuum up both wet and dry things are called vactors.

Vacuum trucks can suck up waste. They also carry water in their tank. The water can wash dirty surfaces. It can thin out a mess for easier vacuuming.

A filter collects pieces of dust. It stays in the vacuum. It doesn't get blown into the air. That way, workers aren't breathing in the dust.

Length:
up to 35 feet
(10.7 m)

Tank Size:
500 to 8,000 gallons
(1,892.7 to 30,283.3 L)

Suction Power:
700 feet
(213.4 m)

Hose Length:
20 to 60 feet
(6.1 to 18.3 m)

JOBSITE TRUCKS

Vacuum Trucks

Sometimes holes need to be dug for poles. Other times, pipes need to be put underground. Water pipes break and need to be fixed. Workers need the ground opened. Vacuum trucks can help! Vacuuming up the dirt is easier and safer than digging.

How does the waste get out of vacuum trucks? Some trucks have a "reverse" button. This pushes everything in the tank out. Others have their tankers emptied like dump trucks.

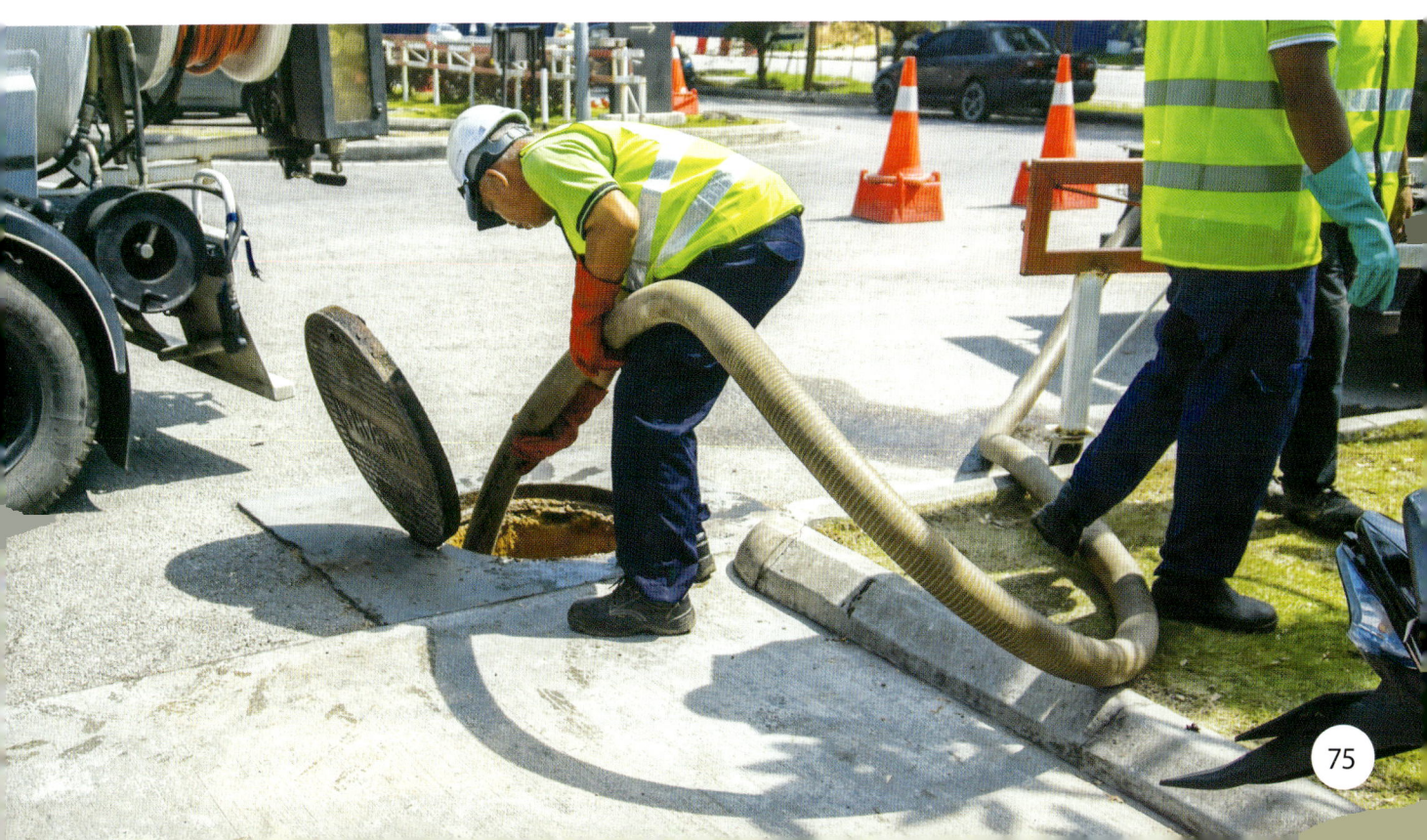

FUN FACT!

Vacuum trucks are how porta potties are emptied!

SPORTS TRUCKS

Big Rig Racing Trucks

Two huge semitrucks line up at the starting line. A timer beeps, and the race starts. Black clouds of smoke fly into the air. Flames shoot out of one of the trucks. The race is on!

FUN FACT! Semitrucks race over short distances less than one mile (1.6 km) long.

Most big rig racers are working trucks. Their drivers keep them in tip-top shape. After the race, they will go back to work hauling things across the country.

Years Made:
1979 to present

Maximum Hp:
2,500 to 3,000 hp

Length:
72 feet
(21.9 m)

Top Speed:
171 miles per hour
(275.2 kmh)

Did You Know?

The big rig racer Shockwave had jet engines strapped to the back. This made it go extra fast!

SPORTS TRUCKS

Monster Trucks

Thousands of people have packed a stadium. A truck with huge wheels bursts in. It's Grave Digger! The truck speeds over a ramp. It flies through the air! The crowd cheers.

Grave Digger

Length: 17 feet (5.2 m)

Maximum Hp: 1,500 hp

Top Speed: 70 miles per hour (112.7 kmh)

Wheel Height: 66 inches (167.6 cm)

Every monster truck is different. Some can sail between 100 and 200 feet (30.5 and 61 m) through the air. Some people race their monster trucks. Others show off their ability to pop up on two wheels.

FUN FACT!

Bigfoot was one of the first, and one of the biggest, monster trucks.

Did You Know?

The first Monster Jam was held in 1992. Trucks race each other on a dirt track. They also perform stunts.

SPORTS TRUCKS

Stadium Super Trucks

Stadium super trucks combine off-road racing with stadium sports. Race car driver Robby Gordon started the Stadium SUPER Trucks series in 2013.

Gordon owns the trucks. Drivers rent them, and Gordon takes care of them. He fixes any damage too.

Each super truck is custom built. But the trucks are all the same. The driver who wins the race has the best skills.

Years Made:
2013 to present

Maximum Hp:
600 hp

Length:
13 feet, 5 inches
(4.1 m)

Top Speed:
140 miles per hour
(225.3 kmh)

FUN FACT!
Some trucks can fly as far as 160 feet (48.8 m) off a jump!

SPORTS TRUCKS

Trophy Trucks

Trophy trucks are built to race off-road. They drive in the dirt. They can drive through deep ruts and sand. They can drive over rocks. And they do it fast!

FUN FACT!

Off-road racing is tough on tires! Trophy trucks carry at least two spares.

Trophy trucks often race through the desert. Special filters keep dust and sand out of their engines. They also race for a long time. They have extra big fuel tanks.

Did You Know?
The Baja 1000 is a race that takes place in Mexico. The route changes every year. Any kind of vehicle can enter. Many racers drive trophy trucks.

Years Made:
1994 to present

Maximum Hp:
525 to 1,000 hp

Top Speed:
150 miles per hour
(241.4 kmh)

Weight:
5,000 to 7,000 pounds
(2,268 to 3,175.1 kg)

SPORTS TRUCKS

Volvo Iron Knight

The World's Fastest Truck

A white blur goes by. Don't blink or you'll miss it! Volvo's Iron Knight is a semitruck. It has broken many speed records. It takes just 4.6 seconds to go from 0 to 60 miles per hour (0 to 96.6 kmh).

Iron Knight is a Volvo FH truck. The FH has computers inside. Most of the computers have been taken out of Iron Knight. This makes the truck lighter and faster.

Volvo Iron Knight

Years Made:
2016 to present

Maximum Hp:
2,400 hp

Top Speed:
171 miles per hour
(275.2 kmh)

Weight:
5 tons
(4.5 metric tons)

FUN FACT!
Boije Ovebrink is Iron Knight's driver. He is a professional truck racer.

SUPER HEAVY TRUCKS

Heavy Haulers

Construction equipment is heavy. Cranes and machines need to be moved to the next jobsite. How do they get there? They are loaded onto heavy haulers with long, flat trailers. A heavy hauler has a lot of power. It can pull those trailers wherever they need to go.

FUN FACT! Heavy haulers can deliver huge things like barns or houses.

Did You Know?
Oversize Load signs are usually required on the front and back of heavy haulers.

Length:
48 to 53 feet
(14.6 to 16.2 m)

Width:
8.5 feet
(2.6 m)

Maximum Load Size:
150,000 to 225,000 pounds
(68,038.9 to 102,058.3 kg)

SUPER HEAVY TRUCKS

Humvees

The United States military needs trucks. Trucks help move troops and cargo. They deliver supplies. The trucks drive through dangerous areas. They need to be tough.

In 1989, the first High Mobility Multipurpose Wheeled Vehicles were ready to drive. They are called Humvees.

FUN FACT! Humvees can be used as ambulances.

Humvees are low and wide. This makes them drive well on rough ground. It is hard to roll one over. Some Humvees have a gun on top. This protects the truck and people inside.

Length:
15 feet
(4.6 m)

Top Speed:
70 miles per hour
(112.7 kmh)

Width:
7 feet
(2.1 m)

Weight:
11,500 pounds
(5,216.3 kg)

SUPER HEAVY TRUCKS

Humvees

Humvees can get dropped right into the action! Helicopters can fly them to where they need to go.

Hills and mountains are no challenge to Humvees. They can climb steep slopes. They can also drive through deep water.

Newer Humvees have special armor. This protects them from dangerous weapons. Ambulance Humvees have bulletproof glass.

Did You Know?
In 1992, Humvees were built for regular people to own. They are called Hummers.

SUPER HEAVY TRUCKS

Road Trains

The Australian Outback is huge. There are few roads. Getting supplies from one end of Australia to the other isn't easy. Road trains make it possible to send huge loads.

Road trains are heavy hauling trucks. They have more than one trailer attached. The small towns and villages along the highways rely on road trains. The nearest store might be many miles away.

Length:
174 feet
(53 m)

Width:
8.5 feet
(2.6 m)

Maximum Load:
220 tons
(199.6 metric tons)

Did You Know?

The world record for the longest road train was set in 2006. A Mack Truck pulled 112 heavy haul trailers. From front to back, it stretched nearly a mile!

TRANSPORTATION TRUCKS

Car Carriers

Cars and trucks need to be brand-new at the car dealership. They can't be driven there from the factory. Car carriers do the job. They carry cars!

Open car carriers can carry two rows of cars. Cars are pushed or driven over a ramp and onto the trailer. Tire straps hold the cars in place. There are no walls or roofs to protect the cars.

FUN FACT!
It can take four to six weeks for a car to get from the factory to a dealership.

Closed carriers keep the cars inside. Cars are safer. They are protected from the weather. They are less likely to be stolen.

Length:
80 feet
(24.4 m)

Width:
8 feet
(2.4 m)

Maximum Load:
80,000 pounds
(36,287.4 kg)

Capacity:
5 to 11 cars

TRANSPORTATION TRUCKS

Chemical Tank Trucks

Liquid can be hard to move. Some liquids are dangerous. Others splash around. Chemical tank trucks can carry liquids safely.

Tank trunks load from either the top or the bottom. Top loaders have a hose at the top of the tank. The liquid is pumped in. Then the liquid is pumped out. It goes into a container.

FUN FACT!

Most trucks that carry liquid have cylinder-shaped tanks. This shape is easier to clean.

Bottom loaders are safer. Valves are turned. Liquid flows in and out.

Length:
43 to 45 feet
(13.1 to 13.7 m)

Width:
8 feet
(2.4 m)

Maximum Load:
1,000 to 11,600 gallons
(3,785.4 to 43,910.8 L)

97

TRANSPORTATION TRUCKS

FUN FACT!
Red flags warn drivers that an oversized load is on the road.

Flatbed Trucks

Flatbed trucks can move heavy loads. They have a wide, flat body. There are no sides or a roof. The load doesn't have to fit exactly on the body. It can hang off the sides.

Some flatbeds can be stretched. Extra-long loads won't hang over.

It is important to secure loads. Tie-downs keep items from flying off of flatbeds.

Did You Know?
Flatbed trucks are very long. They must make wide turns. The longer the truck, the wider the turns.

Length:
48 to 53 feet
(14.6 to 16.2 m)

Width:
8.5 feet
(2.6 m)

Maximum Load:
48,000 pounds
(21,772.4 kg)

TRANSPORTATION TRUCKS

Logging Trucks

Logs need to be carried out of forests. They are delivered to lumber mills. Some logs are carried on stinger-steered pole trailers. They are built to help the truck make turns.

FUN FACT!

Many trucks have a claw that reaches down and grabs the logs. Then it sets them on the truck.

There are also fixed-length log trailers. These trailers do not have a floor. Instead, the logs rest on beams. The trailers can carry tree-length logs. The logs need to be tied down with chains or straps.

Sometimes logs are as wide as the truck. The trucks that haul them are called straight trucks.

Length:
80 feet
(24.4 m)

Width:
8 feet
(2.4 m)

Maximum Load:
80,000 pounds
(36,287.4 kg)

TRANSPORTATION TRUCKS

Oil Tanker Trucks

Oil is used around the world. It is a type of fuel. It is also used to make other items, like plastic. Oil is collected from under Earth's surface. Then it is sent to plants and factories.

Moving oil from one place to another is risky. Oil spills can harm plants and animals. Oil tanker trucks carry oil. They are made from tough materials.

Length:
53 to 100 feet
(16.2 to 30.5 m)

Width:
8 feet
(2.4 m)

Average Load:
8,000 gallons
(30,283.3 L)

Did You Know?
Tanks are divided by walls called baffles. The baffles have holes. They slow down the sloshing liquid when the vehicle is in motion.

Baffles in Liquid Tank

without baffles

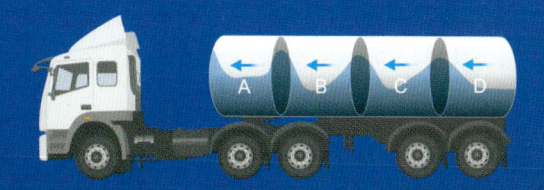

with baffles

TRANSPORTATION TRUCKS

Panel Trucks

Panel trucks were delivery vehicles. The first one was made in 1910. People turned pickups into panel trucks. Businesses painted their names on the sides. They delivered goods.

FUN FACT!
Panel trucks were smaller than vans but were easier to drive.

Panel trucks had high sides and no windows. Some had driver and passenger seats. Others only had room for a driver. Doors on the back could be opened from the outside.

1952 Chevy Panel Truck

Years Made:
1910 to 1968

Length:
19 feet
(5.8 m)

Width:
5 feet
(1.5 m)

Maximum Load:
7,700 pounds
(3,492.7 kg)

TRANSPORTATION TRUCKS

Refrigerated Trucks

Fruits and vegetables come from farms. They have to be delivered to grocery stores. Some food has to travel more than 1,000 miles (1,609.3 km). But people don't want food that is rotten or wilted. How does it stay fresh? Refrigerated trucks!

Length: 15 feet (4.6 m)

Width: 7 feet (2.1 m)

Maximum Load: 44,000 pounds (19,958 kg)

Did You Know?

The first ice cream trucks were built in 1920. They had freezers on board. The ice cream company Good Humor used Ford trucks.

Frederick McKinley Jones was an inventor. He built a refrigerated truck that was sturdy. Food could be delivered from far away. Today, people can eat foods from different states or even different countries!

FUN FACT!

Before Jones's refrigerated truck, produce could only travel around 50 miles (80.5 km) from where it was grown.

TRANSPORTATION TRUCKS

Semitrucks

A semitruck is a truck that is attached to a trailer. Sometimes there is more than one trailer. The trailer can't move on its own. Together, the truck and trailer are called a semitruck or a semi.

FUN FACT!

Another name for semitrucks is 18-wheelers.

Day cabs are smaller than other semis. They are good for short trips. They make deliveries that take a day or less.

Sleeper semis have more room. Drivers can rest or sleep in them. Some sleepers have a bed.

Length:
72 feet
(21.9 m)

Height:
13.5 feet
(4.1 m)

Width:
8.5 feet
(2.6 m)

Maximum Load:
80,000 pounds
(36,287.4 kg)

Did You Know?
A semi drives about 45,000 miles (72,420.5 km) every year.

UNUSUAL TRUCKS

Aircraft Rescue and Fire Fighting Vehicles (ARFFs)

The first water truck for airport fires was built in 1937. The air force used the design to make the first Aircraft Rescue and Fire Fighting Vehicle.

ARFFs must be fast. They must be able to get to an emergency in three minutes or less. They can go from 0 to 50 miles per hour (0 to 80.5 kmh) in 25 seconds. That might seem slow. But they carry a lot of water! They can drive off-road too. Big tires can get the ARFF anywhere it needs to be.

Maximum Length:
36 feet
(11 m)

Height:
13 feet
(4 m)

Maximum Width:
10 feet
(3 m)

Tank Size:
100 to 4,500 gallons
(378.5 to 17,034.4 L)

UNUSUAL TRUCKS

Chevrolet El Camino

Is it a car? Is it a truck? It's an El Camino! The 1959 Chevrolet El Camino was the first car-truck in the United States.

The El Camino was like a truck. It used a station wagon body. This meant the truck bed and the cab were combined. At first, it wasn't popular. In the 1960s, a powerful engine was added. People loved the combined car, truck, and muscle car.

FUN FACT!
In Spanish, *el camino* means "the way."

Years Made:
1959 to 1987

Length:
17 feet
(5.2 m)

Weight:
3,243 pounds
(1,471 kg)

Height:
4.5 feet
(1.4 m)

El Caminos are still on the road today!

UNUSUAL TRUCKS

The DUKW

What has six wheels and can float? DUKWs, or ducks, were first used during World War II. The United States Army wanted them to be like trucks at sea.

FUN FACT! Some cities have duck boat tours. People can see the city. They can take a boat ride too!

The first DUKWs were shaped like a boat. Some of these trucks were built on top of a Jeep. They were called Seeps. *Seep* was short for "seagoing Jeep."

Years Made:
1942 to 1945

Length:
31 feet
(9.4 m)

Top Speed on Water:
5 knots, or 5.7 miles per hour
(9.2 kmh)

Top Speed on Land:
50 miles per hour
(80.5 kmh)

UNUSUAL TRUCKS

Giant Dodge Power Wagon

The Giant Dodge Power Wagon was built in the United Arab Emirates (UAE) in the 1990s. It was based on the 1950 Dodge Power Wagon. But the Giant is 64 times bigger!

The Giant Dodge Power Wagon is more than a car. It's a moving house. There are four bedrooms and a kitchen. The tailgate can be used as a patio.

Length:
62 feet
(18.9 m)

Height:
27 feet
(8.2 m)

Width:
26 feet
(7.9 m)

Weight:
50 tons
(45.4 metric tons)

FUN FACT!

The Dodge Power Wagon was used to explore the desert in the UAE in the 1950s.

UNUSUAL TRUCKS

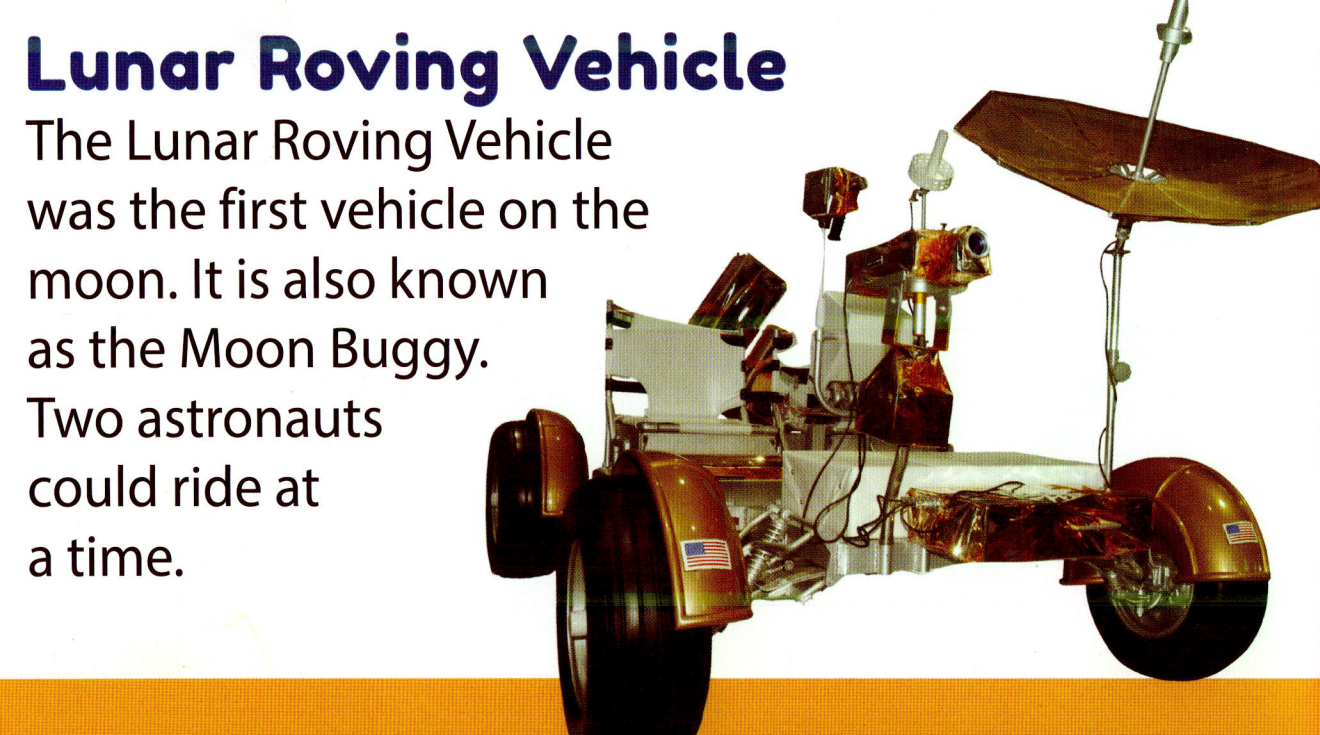

Lunar Roving Vehicle

The Lunar Roving Vehicle was the first vehicle on the moon. It is also known as the Moon Buggy. Two astronauts could ride at a time.

In total, there were four different vehicles. Three were sent to the moon. They are all still on the moon today.

Did You Know?
The fourth buggy was used for testing. It can be seen at the National Air and Space Museum in Washington, DC.

Year Made:
1971

Length:
10 feet
(3 m)

Weight on Earth:
460 pounds
(208.7 kg)

Weight on the Moon:
76 pounds
(34.5 kg)

Top Speed:
8 miles per hour
(12.9 kmh)

UNUSUAL TRUCKS

Off-Road Trucks

Off-roading means driving on anything but paved roads. Jeeps are built for driving on dirt roads. They can go over bumps. Special kits can make them taller. Big tires are easy to add.

FUN FACT!

Rubicon means the Jeep is an off-road model.

Did You Know?
The Gladiator has a removable top and doors.

2023 Jeep Gladiator Rubicon

Jeep's Gladiator Rubicon has all the perks of a Jeep. But it also has a truck bed! It can carry more gear. Drivers can drive to remote places. Then they can hop on a bike to explore more!

Length:
18 feet
(5.5 m)

Width:
6 feet
(1.8 m)

Height:
6 feet
(1.8 m)

Maximum Hp:
285 hp

UNUSUAL TRUCKS

Six-Wheeled Trucks

What's better than four wheels? Six! Trucks with six wheels are also called 6x6 trucks.

The first six-wheeled trucks were made during World War II. The trucks could deliver supplies over rough roads.

FUN FACT! This World War II 6x6 was also called the deuce-and-a-half truck.

There are other trucks with six wheels. They have two in the front and four in the back. The G 63 Mercedes-Benz AMG 6x6 was first used by the Australian Army. Now people take it off-road through deserts, up steep hills, and even down the street.

2023 G 63 Mercedes-Benz AMG 6x6

Length:
19 feet
(5.8 m)

Height:
9 feet
(2.7 m)

Maximum Hp:
536 hp

Width:
7 feet
(2.1 m)

UNUSUAL TRUCKS

Stretch Limo Trucks

Some people want the thrill of a limo. But they also want the roominess of a truck. Around 2003, the first Hummer H2 stretch limo truck was built. Soon, others copied the design.

FUN FACT!
The Hummer H2 stretch limo can hold up to 20 people.

Stretch limos are made by cutting a car in half. They are reconnected with long metal beams. Workers then build the new middle of the truck.

Hummer H2 Stretch Limo

Length:
Can be more than 30 feet (9.1 m)

Height:
6.6 feet (2 m)

Width:
16 feet (4.9 m)

GLOSSARY

aerial
A type of ladder that extends to add extra height.

axle
A rod or shaft that turns a truck's wheels and supports the truck's weight.

bed
The floor or bottom of a truck or trailer.

blade
A flat, wide section of a tool.

box
The enclosed part of a truck that holds cargo.

crane
A truck attachment used to lift or lower heavy objects.

drum
A cylinder attached to the back of a truck.

grapple
An arm with a claw at the end used for lifting and carrying objects.

horsepower
The power an engine produces.

hydraulics
A lifting system that pumps fluid through tubes and cylinders.

lunar
Involving the moon.

payload
The total weight of the cargo and passengers a truck can carry.

valve
A device used to control liquid, gas, and other materials that flow from one area to another.

TO LEARN MORE

More Books to Read

Bolte, Mari. *Forklifts*. Mankato, MN: Creative Education and Creative Paperbacks, 2024.

Collins, Ailynn. *Investigating the Future of Transportation: A Max Axiom Super Science Adventure*. North Mankato, MN: Capstone Press, 2024.

Schamp, Tom. *Wheels: The Big Fun Book of Vehicles*. New York, NY: Prestel Verlag, 2023.

Online Resources

Booklinks
NONFICTION NETWORK
FREE! ONLINE NONFICTION RESOURCES

To learn more about trucks, please visit **abdobooklinks.com** or scan this QR code. These links are routinely monitored and updated to provide the most current information available.

INDEX

electric trucks 9, 42–43, 52

fuel 42, 83, 102–103

military 9, 88, 110, 114, 122, 123

parts 6–7, 15

racing 76–77, 79–83, 85

safety 24, 28, 32, 56, 68, 74, 96–97

self-driving trucks 9, 56–57

tools 15, 31, 33

wheels 6, 7, 8, 19, 23, 36, 62, 71, 78, 79, 108, 114, 122–123

127

PHOTO CREDITS

Cover Photos: 4045/Shutterstock Images, front (tiles); Baloncici/Shutterstock Images, front (tipper truck); Brandon Woyshnis/Shutterstock Images, front (Ford Raptor); Le Do/Shutterstock Images, front (fire truck); Adolf Martinez Soler/Shutterstock Images, back (semitruck)

Interior Photos: Creativa Images/Shutterstock Images, 1, 20, 94; Vitpho/Shutterstock Images, 4 (top), 87 (top), 95; val lawless/Shutterstock Images, 4 (bottom); Projektograf/Shutterstock Images, 5; Rob Wilson/Shutterstock Images, 6–7, 25 (bottom), 46, 96; PixieMe/Shutterstock Images, 7 (top); Sista Vongjintanaruks/Shutterstock Images, 7 (bottom); S. Candide/Shutterstock Images, 8 (top), 36, 72; Erik Laan/Shutterstock Images, 8 (middle); James K. Troxell/Shutterstock Images, 8 (bottom), 38; jon lyall/Shutterstock Images, 9 (top), 111; Adolf Martinez Soler/Shutterstock Images, 9 (middle), 48; Mike Mareen/Shutterstock Images, 9 (bottom), 43; StockPhotosArt/Shutterstock Images, 10; sakoat contributor/Shutterstock Images, 11; bit mechanic/Shutterstock Images, 12; SPK Studio Images/Shutterstock Images, 13; ASP-media/Shutterstock Images, 14; fotorobs/Shutterstock Images, 15; Vadim Ratnikov/Shutterstock Images, 16; Bapak Dedi Setiawan/Shutterstock Images, 17 (top); Samuel Acosta/Shutterstock Images, 17 (bottom); TFoxFoto/Shutterstock Images, 18, 35 (bottom), 100; Philip Arno Photography/Shutterstock Images, 19 (top); Robert Pernell/Shutterstock Images, 19 (bottom); Mr. Tempter/Shutterstock Images, 21 (top); AliaksaB/Shutterstock Images, 21 (bottom); bondgrunge/Shutterstock Images, 22; Alex Sobal/Shutterstock Images, 23; Ian Dewer Photography/Shutterstock Images, 24; Marzolino/Shutterstock Images, 25 (top); Nikita Minaev/Shutterstock Images, 26; kontur-vid/Shutterstock Images, 27 (top); Yuri Schmidt/Shutterstock Images, 27 (bottom); Michael Derrer Fuchs/Shutterstock Images, 28; SviatlanaLaza/Shutterstock Images, 29 (top); Jerald LaOrange/Shutterstock Images, 29 (bottom); Toa55/Shutterstock Images, 30; Azami Adiputera/Shutterstock Images, 31 (top); kevin brine/Shutterstock Images, 31 (bottom); TLF/Shutterstock Images, 32; Lucian Coman/Shutterstock Images, 33 (top); CameraCraft/Shutterstock Images, 33 (bottom); Valentin Valkov/Shutterstock Images, 34; Krasula/Shutterstock Images, 35 (top); Sergey Kohl/Shutterstock Images, 37, 110; Dmitry Eagle Orlov/Shutterstock Images, 39; Free Wind 2014/Shutterstock Images, 40; Lasting Shutter Studio/Shutterstock Images, 41; Jonathan Weiss/Shutterstock Images, 42, 51; Alden Jewel via Flickr, 44; Wirestock Creators/Shutterstock Images, 45; nitinut380/Shutterstock Images, 47; Philip Lange/Shutterstock Images, 49, 91 (top), 116; betto rodrigues/Shutterstock Images, 50; Cover Images/Zuma Press/Newscom, 52; arda savasciogullari/Shutterstock Images, 53; enot-poloskun/iStock/Getty Images Plus, 54; Alin Popescu/Shutterstock Images, 55; Imagine China/Newscom, 56; Scharfsinn/Shutterstock Images, 57, 85; prochasson frederic/Shutterstock Images, 58; Lester Balajadia/Shutterstock Images, 59; Susan B Sheldon/Shutterstock Images, 60; Tim Daugherty/Shutterstock Images, 61; Shotshop GmbH/Alamy Stock Photo, 62; Joshua Rainey Photography/Shutterstock Images, 63; stefan11/Shutterstock Images, 64; wavebreakmedia/Shutterstock Images, 65; Bernd Rehorst/Shutterstock Images, 66 (top); Oporty786/Shutterstock Images, 66 (bottom); ungvar/Shutterstock Images, 67, 74; Zhak Yaroslav Photo/Getty Images, 68; Tricky_Shark/Shutterstock Images, 69; picturepixx/Shutterstock Images, 70; Maria Dryfhout/Shutterstock Images, 71; Nolichuckyjake/Shutterstock Images, 73; Veniamin Kraskov/Shutterstock Images, 75 (top); kiraziku2u/Shutterstock Images, 75 (bottom); bsankow/Shutterstock Images, 76; Santiparp Wattanaporn/Shutterstock Images, 77; BW Press/Shutterstock Images, 78; Michael Stokes/Shutterstock Images, 79; Jon Nicholls Photography/Shutterstock Images, 80, 81; alexkoral/Shutterstock Images, 82; Stan Sholik/Zuma Press/Newscom, 83; NearEMPTiness/Wikimedia Commons, 84; Larry Jordan/Dreamstime.com, 86; aappp/Shutterstock Images, 87 (bottom); Jarod Grey/Shutterstock Images, 88; PhotoStock10/Shutterstock Images, 89 (top); StockPhotosLV/Shutterstock Images, 89 (bottom); Kirk Wester/Shutterstock Images, 90; Art Konovalov/Shutterstock Images, 91 (bottom), 124–125; John Carnemolla/Shutterstock Images, 92–93; Mino Surkala/Shutterstock Images, 93; Praethip Docekalova/Shutterstock Images, 97; Tom Robertson/Shutterstock Images, 98; Stephen Dewhurst/Shutterstock Images, 99; Irina Borsuchenko/Shutterstock Images, 101; Vytautas Kielaitis/Shutterstock Images, 102; Graphic_BKK1979/Getty Images, 103; Gestalt Imagery/Shutterstock Images, 104, 112–113, 113; Ken Morris/Shutterstock Images, 105; Gualberto Becerra/Shutterstock Images, 106; Darren Brode/Shutterstock Images, 107 (top); USDA.gov/Wikimedia Commons, 107 (bottom); View Apart/Shutterstock Images, 108; graham tomlin/Shutterstock Images, 109; Aaron of L.A. Photography/Shutterstock Images, 114 (top); GagliardiPhotography/Shutterstock Images, 114 (bottom); 2p2play/Shutterstock Images, 115; Leena Robinson/Shutterstock Images, 117; HUM Images/Contributor/Getty Images, 118 (top); Edwin Verin/Shutterstock Images, 118 (bottom); Natasa Ivancev/Shutterstock Images, 119; Arnold O. A. Pinto/Shutterstock Images, 120; Boykov/Shutterstock Images, 121; NYC Russ/Shutterstock Images, 122; Sport car hub/Shutterstock Images, 123; Dasfa/Zjah/Wenn.com/Newscom, 125

MAIN LIBRARY